SUPER SANDCASTLE™
It's the Alphabet!

It's O!

Oona Gaarder-Juntti

Consulting Editor, Diane Craig, M.A./Reading Specialist

ABDO Publishing Company

Published by ABDO Publishing Company, 8000 West 78th Street, Edina, Minnesota 55439. Copyright © 2010 by Abdo Consulting Group, Inc. International copyrights reserved in all countries. No part of this book may be reproduced in any form without written permission from the publisher. Super SandCastle™ is a trademark and logo of ABDO Publishing Company.

Printed in the United States.
♺ PRINTED ON RECYCLED PAPER

Editor: Pam Price
Content Developer: Nancy Tuminelly
Cover and Interior Design and Production: Kelly Doudna, Mighty Media
Photo Credits: iStockphoto (Jani Bryson), Shutterstock
Hula Hoop® is a registered trademark of WHAM-O Inc.

Library of Congress Cataloging-in-Publication Data
Gaarder-Juntti, Oona, 1979-
 It's O! / Oona Gaarder-Juntti.
    p. cm. -- (It's the alphabet!)
 ISBN 978-1-60453-602-7
 1. English language--Alphabet--Juvenile literature. 2. Alphabet books--Juvenile literature. I. Title.
 PE1155.G2939 2010
 421'.1--dc22
 ⟨E⟩
                        2009022025

Super SandCastle™ books are created by a team of professional educators, reading specialists, and content developers around five essential components—phonemic awareness, phonics, vocabulary, text comprehension, and fluency—to assist young readers as they develop reading skills and strategies and increase their general knowledge. All books are written, reviewed, and leveled for guided reading, early reading intervention, and Accelerated Reader® programs for use in shared, guided, and independent reading and writing activities to support a balanced approach to literacy instruction.

About SUPER SANDCASTLE™

Bigger Books for Emerging Readers
Grades K–4

Created for library, classroom, and at-home use, Super SandCastle™ books support and engage young readers as they develop and build literacy skills and will increase their general knowledge about the world around them. Super SandCastle™ books are an extension of SandCastle™, the leading preK–3 imprint for emerging and beginning readers. Super SandCastle™ features a larger trim size for more reading fun.

Let Us Know
Super SandCastle™ would like to hear your stories about reading this book. What was your favorite page? Was there something hard that you needed help with? Share the ups and downs of learning to read. We want to hear from you! Send us an e-mail.

sandcastle@abdopublishing.com

Contact us for a complete list of SandCastle™, Super SandCastle™, and other nonfiction and fiction titles from ABDO Publishing Company.

www.abdopublishing.com • 8000 West 78th Street
Edina, MN 55439 • 800-800-1312 • 952-831-1632 fax

Aa Bb Cc Dd Ee
Ff Gg Hh Ii Jj Kk
Ll Mm Nn Oo Pp
Qq Rr Ss Tt Uu Vv
Ww Xx Yy Zz

The Letter Oo

O and o can also look like

Oo **Oo** Oo Oo Oo Oo

The letter o is a vowel.

It is the 15th letter of the alphabet.

short o as in frog

frog

A capital O looks the same as a lowercase o except that it's bigger.

Molly's frog Oscar often hops on a long box.

box

long o as in r**o**se

pony

Logan goes home and shows his pony a rose.

rose

7

o as in c**o**ins and t**o**ys

toys

coins

8

boy

The boy spends his coins
on toys that make noise.

9

o as in wh**o** and b**oo**ts

rooster

boots

movie

The rooster who went to the movie had cool boots.

o as in **out** and c**o**w

cow

ground

12

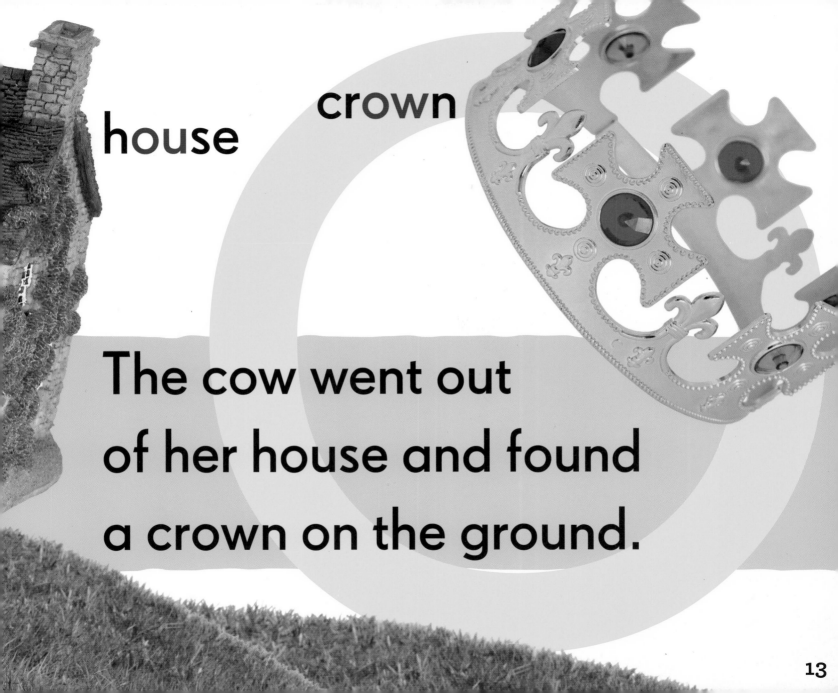

house

crown

The cow went out
of her house and found
a crown on the ground.

14

Otto the owl lives alone in an old oak tree.

When the moon comes out,
he enjoys a cup of tea.

Otto is lonely and longs for one loyal friend.

He hopes for someone to talk to,
a friend on whom he can depend.

Otto often hoots,
"Hoo, hoo. Who is there?"

No one ever answers, but Otto does not care.

Otto has the courage
to leave home and go explore.

He meets a rooster named Rocky
who lives in the house next door.

18

Rocky invites him over
for mushroom and onion soup.

Rocky shows Otto his toys,
and together they Hula Hoop.

Rocky the rooster is a good friend
through and through.

Now when Otto hoots,
Rocky crows, "Cock-a-doodle-do!"

21

Which words have the same **o** sound as h**o**p?

frog

robin

rose

coin

box

rooster

rocket

dog

23

Glossary

courage (p. 18) – the strength to help yourself or others, even if you are afraid.

crow (p. 20) – to make the sharp, shrill cry of a rooster.

depend (p. 16) – to trust or rely on.

explore (p. 18) – to travel in order to learn about other places.

Hula Hoop (p. 19) – to use a Hula Hoop. A Hula Hoop is a brand of plastic hoop that is twirled around the body.

invite (p. 19) – to ask someone to do something or go somewhere with you.

lonely (p. 16) – feeling sad and alone.

loyal (p. 16) – faithful and honest.

mushroom (p. 19) – an umbrella-shaped fungus used in cooking.

To promote letter recognition, letters are highlighted instead of glossary words in this series. The page numbers above indicate where the glossary words can be found.

More Words with O

Find the **o** in the beginning, middle, or end of each word.

about	doll	off	ought	school
book	goat	oil	our	touch
close	hello	only	oven	tractor
coat	hole	open	own	work
cookie	lion	or	ox	yellow
could	no	orange	question	you